YOU DON'T HAVE TO BELIEVE TO BELONG

Like, for real.

AARON BREWER

Copyright © 2021 Aaron Brewer

YOU DON'T HAVE TO BELIEVE TO BELONG

Published by Fresh Faith

ISBN 9798517983831

All rights reserved.

Except for brief excerpts for review purposes, no part of this book may be reproduced or used in any form without written permission from the author.

All Scripture quotations are taken from the Christian Standard Bible®, Copyright © 2020 by Holman Bible Publishers®. Used by permission. Christian Standard Bible® and CSB® are federally registered trademarks of Holman Bible Publishers.

Author photo by Kara Cunningham, Captured Memories by KC Photography.

To order additional copies of this resource, visit *FreshFaith.org*.

To my wife, Andrea, who has been my faithful companion on this wildly beautiful journey of faith. You are the encouragement that made this work possible, and you are the voice that made this dream a reality. You are God's tangible grace to me, and I am forever deeply grateful to love you.

CONTENTS

5	Dedication
9	Me & Religon
15	Judas & Jesus
21	Questions & Answers
31	Grass & Gratitude
39	Community & Identity
51	Pain & Passion
77	Theory & Theology
87	Faith & Feelings
103	Baggage & Belonging
115	Connect with Aaron

ONE
ME & RELIGION

A gentle breeze was blowing through her silky brown hair as she gazed over the vast ocean, beautifully kissed with the pink and orange hues of a summer sunrise. A warm mug of coffee wrapped in her hand, three little daughters and a husband still asleep in the house behind her, she was in the very presence of God. And she knew it. She soaked it in. She lived it to the fullest. She allowed this moment to transcend her day as she poured out God's presence she had bottled that morning into every stranger and loved one she encountered, leaving them a little better than she found them. That night when her head finally rested on the pillow and her eyes gently shut, she rested in gratitude for the gift of participating in the presence of God that day.

That woman, her name is Andrea. She's my wife. She has transformed the way I see and encounter God today. I see and experience God through my wife, my kids, nature, humanity, and my life. But that's not how I've always encountered God.

The Early Days

I grew up in the religion of Christianity. Different from the relationship I have with God now as a Jesus follower, my childhood was plagued with the stale legalism of Christian religion. I went to a Christian academy from kindergarten through twelfth grade. If you're counting, that's thirteen years. Because my family were also members of the church that owned the academy, I was on the church premises six or seven days a week.

As a child, the goal of my influencers was for me to make a commitment to Jesus - to get "saved." So I did at the ripe old age of five. Following that prayer of salvation was a baptism. Then I went to Sunday School and learned as many Bible verses as I possibly could. The more Bible verses I knew, the more I was growing as a Christian - at least that's the way it was supposed to work.

As a teenager, the preachers would say whatever they needed to in order to get me to doubt that I was indeed saved and going to heaven. If they succeeded, I would raise my hand, go to the altar and pray for salvation, and they would add a number to their ministry scoreboard. I remember having a bonfire one Wednesday night for our youth service, and we were told to bring all of our secular albums, t-shirts, posters, and any other items that weren't honoring to God so we could throw them in the fire. And that's exactly what I did. I'm pretty sure the goal of my church leaders for me in high school was to keep me from drinking, smoking, and having sex. Those were the big three. Of course, cursing and associating with troublemakers was frowned upon too.

For the most part, I thought I turned out decently through the eyes of my church. I graduated from the academy with honors and decided to pursue full time ministry. I went straight to Bible school, then graduated college with a degree in pastoral ministry. I even married a preacher's daughter, so I thought the church was probably pleased that they had crafted a fine Christian man who was now serving on staff at his father-in-law's church across town.

Not even close - I was dead wrong. In fact, I learned that even when I got it right and did all the things I was taught to do and supposed to do, I was still wrong, and I didn't belong. I belonged when it was convenient and easy for them, but it was uncomfortable for my spiritual leaders that I was now serving in a church that was affiliated with another denomination. Both denominations are Christian, by the way, which is why I found my sudden displacement a bit confusing.

No longer finding a place to belong in the familiar circle of community I came from did open my eyes though. I began to question what I was taught about God as a child. I thought, "If God loves all of us as much as they say, and God is in us both, how can they be against me just because I'm not with them?

Maybe the God they taught me about isn't who God really is at all."

I then set out on a journey that changed everything and gave me endless hope and the fullest life and the deepest love. A journey that led me to the wonderful realization that I actually do belong. And so do you.

The Method

Growing up I was taught a method that most traditional Christians unconsciously adhere to: believe, behave, belong. In that order. After you believe like us, you will then behave like us, and when you behave like us, you will then belong with us.

More modern Christians who are progressive teach a new methodology in order to reach unchurched people: belong, believe, behave. You have a place to belong with us so that you'll believe like us, which then causes you to behave like us. Although this seems to jive better with the life Jesus lived and offered to others who followed him, I still see a hidden agenda involved. It's a bait and switch, because the goal is still the same - believe and behave like me.

Jesus lived and loved with no agenda, the goal was belonging with no strings attached. Like the disciple Judas, even those who would never believe in Jesus still found a place to belong with him. It's not that Jesus didn't desire or invite people to believe in him; it's that their belief didn't change their innate belonging.

Jesus showed us that there is no method. It's belong, belong, belong. He showed us that God loves us and accepts us no matter what we do, who we are, or what we believe. You don't have to believe to belong.

Aaron Brewer

TWO
JUDAS & JESUS

In April of 2018, my wife, Andrea, and I started a church in our hometown of Winchester, Virginia, with about seven other families. Our slogan was *You Don't Have to Believe to Belong*. I took so much heat for that slogan from other religious people in our community. I had a friend tell me one day to go listen to the latest sermon from a church that was right beside my neighborhood. I was listening while on a run, and I happened to be running through that church's parking lot when I heard the pastor (whom I had never met) start talking in my ears about "a false church in the area that advertises using the slogan *You Don't Have to Believe to Belong* to lure people in." His sermon title that day was "Yes, You Do Have to Believe to Belong."

As our church was launching, I received countless emails and messages from concerned Christians in the community asking what I meant exactly by our slogan. My response was always the same: "What we mean when we say, *You Don't Have to Believe to Belong* is you don't have to believe to belong."

For us, there were no strings attached to belonging, and I realized later why so many religious people had issues with our slogan. Embracing it would've meant they no longer had control over what others' spiritual journeys would look like, so they feared possible diversity. They would use the Bible to form a case against us, but you know as well as I do that you can use the Bible to justify anything and support any story you want to tell.

It's funny, really. I never received one negative inquiry from a non-Jesus follower. All of the targeted questions and concerns came from religious people, people who were Christians. I found this revealing to the nature of religion. When we are part of a religious community defined by what we believe, any variance from that belief system becomes a threat to the purity of the community, and we become what Brené Brown calls "sorted."[1] Sorting is dangerous, because it presents diversity as a threat and creates fear as the mode of operation, not love. It develops the corrosive inner dialogue that if you're not with us, you're against us (which is the exact opposite of what Jesus said in Mark 9:40, "For whoever is not against us is for us.")

Why are Christians so exclusive when Jesus was so inclusive?

---

[1] Brown, Brené, Braving the Wilderness: The Quest for True Belonging and the Courage to Stand Alone. New York: Random House, 2017.

The reason I never received a question or a concern from a non-Jesus follower is because having a place to belong with no strings attached sounds like a great place to be. And it's true, with Jesus is always a great place to be.

So I decided we would always err on the side of humanity since Jesus laid down his life for them. That means we have a seat at our table for humanity, no matter who you are, where you come from, what you have, what you don't have, what you did, who you love, or what you believe (or don't).

Jesus is the Lens

There is a lens that I use to view all of the Bible through. It's the lens of who Jesus is. Jesus is the full expression of God's heart wrapped in flesh and sent to us, not to show us the way to heaven, but to show us who we were meant to be all along. There's a reason that in every major religion Jesus is highly respected. He is full of love and truth delivered in grace and peace. So when I read the Bible, it doesn't tell me who God is; rather, God revealed through the life of Jesus tells me what the Bible means. There are some really difficult passages in the Bible about unjust murder on behalf of God, among other terrible things that are attributed to God. These things don't tell me who God is, but who God is tells me how to understand these things.

When Jesus becomes our lens we read the Bible through, all of it comes alive and is applicable to our every moment. Although God was the inspiration of all scripture, it wasn't orally dictated by God. Humanity's interactions with God and understanding of God influenced the way it was written. The Bible was written by humans for humans. God was certainly involved, but probably not in the way we have imagined. For instance, God is certainly involved in my writing this book, but I'm not taking oral dictation from the Almighty by any stretch of the imagination. Instead, my journey with God has prompted me to write about God for humanity. I am in no way comparing the inspiration of the Bible to my writing, but understanding the inspiration process may help us approach the Bible better. The word literally means "God-breathed". But did God breathe the actual words of the Bible into the authors' ears, or did He breathe life into the words as he influenced the authors who wrote of their experiences and understanding of the Almighty? That's why Jesus is the only lens through which the Bible makes sense and becomes transformative. He is the constant truth of love that is the lens through which all of scripture must be filtered in order to bring it to life. Why? Because Jesus is the very word - or *breath* - of God who is the source of all life (see John 1).

Judas is the Example

My immediate reaction to personal attacks from religious folks for my spiritual beliefs is to point to Jesus. When I take a look at the life of Jesus to point to an example of not having to believe to belong, I go straight to Judas.

Judas was the disciple infamously known for betraying Jesus, selling him out for thirty pieces of silver to his enemies, ultimately leading to the murder of Jesus.

Judas was also the treasurer of Jesus' ministry, making him the only disciple with an official role and title. Judas belonged.

In John 13:18-30, Jesus gives us the greatest example of belonging when he predicts that Judas will betray him. We know from the timeline expressed in Luke 22 that Jesus has already served what we now call *communion* at the last supper. He explained that the bread they were eating represented his body that would be broken for them, and he explained that the wine they were drinking represented his blood that would be shed for them. After explaining the significance of those elements being his sacrifice for humanity, they all took and ate and drank, participating in this moment together. After being prompted by John to answer who will betray him, Jesus then took the bread (representing his body) and dipped it in the wine (representing his blood) and personally served it to Judas.

Do you see the powerful significance of that?

Jesus has just expressed how deep and sorrowful his death would be, but that it would bring hope and life for humanity through it. After using the bread and wine to describe it, he serves them personally only to Judas. We read that Jesus knew Judas was about to go and betray him literally seconds later. And Jesus, knowing that, is saying to Judas in that moment through serving him communion, "Even though you don't believe in me and will betray me, and I will die because of your act, even in this moment, *especially* because of this moment, my sacrifice is for you too, and you belong here." Judas never believed. Judas never behaved. But Judas always belonged. And so do we all.

THREE QUESTIONS & ANSWERS

Let me be as honest as I can be. I'm a preacher, and I still have questions about God and faith and life and everything else every single day. I don't mean questions that are for more mature people in the faith, whatever that means. I wrestle with the same questions you probably have.

Who is God really?

Does God have a hand in everything in the world? Anything?

Are my prayers really heard by the Creator?

Can I call him the Creator? Or is Originator better?

Wait. Is God a him or a her, or neither? Or both?

There are so many more questions I have and ask. No matter how much I learn about God, and no matter how close I sometimes feel to God, some questions still surface every once in a while, and that's not a bad thing. A faith that can't be questioned is a faith that can't be trusted. A God who's not big enough for my questions is a God who's too small for my faith.

Wisdom, Not Answers

One thing I've come to understand on my faith journey is that if I come looking for answers, I'll never be satisfied; but if I come looking for wisdom, I'll always be satisfied. While answers are definitive to the questions at hand, wisdom transcends questions and invites participation.

I don't know about you, but I was told all of the answers I needed for life were in the Bible. When I had a question about why bad things happen or a struggle with what to do in a relationship, my spiritual leaders would say, "What does the Bible say? Life is an open book test, and all the answers are in the book [Bible]."

Well, they aren't.

But that's not negative, it's actually extremely helpful. If we were supposed to find answers in the Bible, our faith would be stagnant, dull, and informative. Lucky for us we can find wisdom in the Bible, which makes our faith fluid, exciting, unique, and transformative. When I stopped looking for answers and started looking for wisdom, I had a newfound and freeing purpose for reading the Bible, and my faith came alive.

When I approach the Bible looking for wisdom, it invites me to participate in the story of God through my own life. It allows me to see the wisdom of God in someone else's story and use it in my own, elevating the way I live and transforming who I am. I can take that wisdom and use it in multiple circumstances I go through, as opposed to finding a single answer to a single question. Wisdom gives the Bible a seat at my modern table, making the vintage text relevant to my life today. The opposite is also true. A Bible that's only full of answers makes the text archaic and irrelevant, answering questions we're no longer asking.

Answers stop a journey where wisdom continues a journey. Once you find the answer, that's the end. But that's not how the Bible works. The Bible teaches wisdom through poetry, history, fiction, non-fiction, biography and more. The Bible gives us the opportunity to explore its depths and palettes, mining wisdom that is fuel to continue on to whatever adventure is next on our journey.

The Freedom of Ignorance

It's funny how questions are often the space that separates people from connecting with God. As a minister I've had many people tell me, "I'd be open to God if someone would tell me why suffering in the world exists or where God came from." What they're really saying is, "I have unanswered questions that stand between me and God, and they need to be reconciled first."

The reason I think it's funny is because there is no good answer to some of the ominous questions we have. The only honest answer any human can give is, "I don't know." The irony is that being comfortable with unanswered questions can often lead us face to face with God. So not only do questions have the ability to keep us from seeing God, they also have the ability to open our eyes to see God. The difference is whether or not we need the answer.

Not only is, "I don't know," an honest answer, but it's also fully liberating. We don't have to know the answer, we aren't expected to know the answer, and that's okay. When we give ourselves the grace to say, "I don't know," we free ourselves from the burden of knowing. Let God carry the burden of knowing the answer; you were never built to carry it.

There was a classmate in my British Literature class in college who would say this phrase: "If ignorance is bliss, I'm blistered." I love that phrase. It's our ignorance that frees us to live life without fear. Like a child who is too young to understand the danger of leaping into the air from the top step of a staircase in the direction of her father's arms, we live fearlessly and leap knowing we can fly when we are too ignorant to be scared of falling. Ignorance of things we were never meant to understand can be a gift that gives us the freedom to live without fear.

You Don't Have To Believe To Belong

My dad is one of my favorite people on the planet. He's one of those guys people love and love to be around. His friends often say that if I were to write a book of incidents that have happened to my dad, it would be a best-seller comedy. If you followed him around with a camera, you could make a reality TV show that would have insanely high ratings. He's just clumsy, hilarious, passionate, unaware, opinionated, and easily offended. Being in his life is hysterical. It's always a blast when you're with my dad.

There was a time when the United States government was facing a shutdown due to the refusal of bipartisanship. My dad was glued to the news. I was glued to three little girls I couldn't let out of my sight.

My dad called me.

Me: "Hello?"

Dad: "Well, what are we gonna do?"

Me: "About what?"

Dad: "About what! Government shutdown, that's what!"

And just like that the conversation was over and he hung up. Don't worry, he wasn't mad. My dad doesn't start or end phone conversations; he just picks up in the middle of a conversation you were never having and hangs up when he's finished talking.

I talked to him a bit later, and he shared with me his thoughts on the whole matter. He also shared every horrific and possible outcome that he heard the news anchor share - verbatim. And I told him I had no idea what he was talking about, as this was the first I'd heard of it. He was so shocked. I told him that I was really glad to be ignorant of the news, because while he was so intensely stressed about what the next week's economy would look like for his business, my only stress was about peanut butter getting on the couch from Avie's face. Avie is our baby girl and our messiest eater.

While I know the value of staying informed to be responsibly prepared, I also know the priceless value and joyous freedom selective ignorance can offer.

Selective ignorance is necessary for some of our big questions concerning God and life. It gives us the freedom to live life to the fullest without the limits of fear and certainty.

Did you catch that? Certainty can be just as limiting to your life as fear. When things are uncertain, it gives us the opportunity to step forward in faith, trusting God for what's next. Living with a healthy measure of uncertainty doesn't wreck our lives when something unexpected happens, because we were never certain of what was ahead anyway. A lot of our stress comes from our reality being different from our expectations. When we're certain about the future, it gives us false security that limits our ability to live every moment to fullest. Although certainty and security seem like they would offer stability, they actually keep us from experiencing the hope and freedom that comes from not having to be in control. There is an advantage to uncertainty as it relates to all of the questions we think we need to be certain about before engaging a relationship with God. Certainty can be a trap, and uncertainty can be a gift.

Who Not What

Questions are a big deal in our culture. So are answers. Jobs start with an interview of questions and answers. Friendships grow from questions and answers. Marriages form because questions and answers were a major component of a series of dates. And when we tell someone about an engagement, the phrases used are either, "he popped the question," or, "she said yes!" Buying a home consists of questions and answers involving the buyer, seller, agent, and lender. Buying a car is the result of good questions and shifty answers. Doctor visits start with a million questions, and only a few are actually about you. Education is measured by answers to specific questions. Our whole culture is totally dependent upon what questions are asked and what answers are given.

So why would our faith journey be any different? For most people, it's not. It's all about a measurement of information. I would argue that although questions are essential, answers are relative. I know we don't like to use the term relative when it comes to faith, but that's really the only word that's actually a true representation of a unique faith journey that's specifically yours. All journeys don't look the same; they're not supposed to. That makes some of our answers relative, per se.

Asking questions should never corrode our faith; rather, asking questions should enhance our faith. Not because we have more answers, but because we're engaging our faith. I've actually found that the more questions I have, the less answers I end up with, but the more fulfilled I am in my journey. It's when we can't ask questions or don't ask questions that we become stuck in a toxic cycle of faith that only exploration and discovery through questions can untangle.

Most faith questions aren't asked with a motivation of exploration and discovery. Most faith questions are asked to figure out either what you believe or what someone else believes. And the answers we give formulate what we believe. In fact, if you were to ask about the differences of the major religions in the world, what they believe would be what differentiates them. If you were to ask about the differences of all the denominations within Christianity, what they believe would be what differentiates them. That's why we feel it's important to figure out what we believe, so we know where we belong.

The different beliefs of Christians, all based on the same Bible, are as numerous as the species on planet Earth. And if we're trying to figure out what beliefs are actually right and our entire future is depending on it, we'd drive ourselves crazy - and most of us quite literally have. That's why each denomination is so adamant about their doctrine and theology, because they fear others who don't believe like them don't belong with God. Granted, they caveat this with displaying essential and non-essential beliefs, but there is still a line drawn somewhere that says you don't belong. Surprisingly, I'm not against denominations; they're a great structure for the long term security of the church and outreach. My issue, however, comes with the dogma of theological arrogance that promotes exclusion rather than inclusion.

What if our faith journey isn't supposed to be about what we believe? What if our spiritual maturity and relationship with God isn't formed by what we believe at all? What if *Who* we believe is more important than *what* we believe?

I'm a Jesus-follower, so I believe in who Jesus represented God to be through his love, grace, compassion, and mercy. However, I'm also aware that not everyone reading my words follows Jesus or identifies with Christianity, so let me make this applicable to you. There is one God. If there are multiple Gods, they would, by definition, stop being God, because one would have to be most powerful in order to actually be God. God is seen through many lights: love, joy, peace, patience, kindness, goodness, faithfulness, gentleness, and self-control - just to name a few. Humanity is crafted in the image of God, meaning God can be seen in and through us when we become those traits that can only come from God in us. So to believe in God is to believe in love, to believe in joy, and so on, as they are who God is. And those colors of God are made visible through humanity.

That's why *Who* you believe is greater than *what* you believe. What you believe is intangible, it's just an idea. But Who you believe demands participation in making God's presence a reality. What you believe is informational, but Who you believe is transformational. For me, that's Jesus. He embodies and participates in all of Who God is. I believe Jesus is the very heart of God, made human, to show us not only Who God is, but who we were meant to be. He came to humanity for humanity, not just for a group of humanity. Jesus presented God to be an all inclusive gift of endless love for humanity, based on the performance of Jesus instead of the performance of humanity. So when I have tough questions that I don't know the answers to, I take comfort and hope in knowing that even if I don't get it right, God already loves me enough to give me Jesus, the very heart of God. And because I have the heart of God, I don't need all the answers to believe, and I don't need the performance of a lifetime to belong. I just get to be fully known and fully loved by God, while loving others and loving life.

FOUR
GRASS &
GRATITUDE

Have you ever felt like God isn't present in the world, much less in your life? Maybe you've wanted to engage a relationship with God or hoped something like that existed, but you could never see God or justify God's presence in your life and circumstances. It makes it difficult to fully engage with a Supreme Being who is supposed to be inherently good while nothing in your life seems to be good. It's also difficult to see human suffering and natural disaster while trying to make a case for the existence or care of God. And if a God who could prevent such suffering and disaster does exist but does nothing about it, who would want to know and love that God? I mean, that's the stuff pure evil is made of - knowing one could intervene but watches for pleasure instead.

Trust me when I tell you I've heard all the rebuttals.

God is in control.

It's all a part of God's plan.

You can't question God.

God is still sovereign.

God's ways are higher than ours.

True? Maybe in some way, shape, or form, but not here. The shallow use of the Bible as a tool to make excuses for God is pathetic. Nevertheless, it makes it difficult to want to see God in anything when everything around you is in turmoil and pain. When you can't pay your bills, your mom just died, your child is strung out, your spouse has left, your cancer is back, your car is broken, the pantry is empty, and you just opened an eviction notice, it's hard to see God in the middle of your mess.

Frame It with Gratitude

Gratitude is the key that unlocks every blessing in your life. Now before you think I'm getting all prosperity on you, rest assured, I'm not. I'm not saying that when you're thankful, all of the sudden your bills are paid, your cancer is gone, and new blessings start flooding into your life. What I am saying is that when you frame your circumstances with gratitude, your curses become blessings.

God, I know I can't pay my bills, but I'm grateful I have eyes to see the bill and intelligence enough to read and understand it.

God, I'm sad about my mom dying, but I'm grateful for the years I had with her and the love she gave me.

God, my kid is strung out, but I'm thankful they're still alive for me to love. Thank you for hope that still exists for them.

I could go on, but I think you get the point. When you frame anything with gratitude, it becomes a blessing. Gratitude is the lens that brings color to life and perspective to circumstance. And when you're deep in the middle of big, messy circumstances, what you need is a higher and better perspective.

Practicing gratitude offers us a reflective clarity that has the power to change our reality through our attitude. When Andrea and I have had a frustrating argument, it's easy for me to filter every little thing she says or does through that frustration. When she's washing the dishes I left by the sink, my frustration from earlier tells me that she's doing it out of spite to prove she always has to clean up after me. In reality, she's just washing the dishes. But my attitude tells me a false narrative. Practicing gratitude changes how I approach my wife throughout the day beyond our argument so that my attitude is grateful and not hateful. When I have a grateful attitude, I can see the truth clearly in front of me that I otherwise would not have seen. Sometimes when we argue, I remind myself that I'm grateful to have a wife to argue with who loves me and our children. Also, I'm grateful our relationship is healthy enough to be a safe space to openly share different opinions and feelings and still know we're loved no matter what. Gratitude has the power to change the reality of the rest of my day when my attitude could have been shaped by frustration instead.

Gratitude is extremely healthy, liberating, and necessary; it creates a space to belong. It lets you belong with yourself, even in a mess. It lets others belong with you, even through an argument. You can create the space of belonging through your gratitude.

Everything in your life becomes better when you're thankful. Everything. Your approach matters, and gratitude is always the right approach. It's not so much about what's happening to you, but how you approach it and what you do with it. Approach life with thankfulness and frame it with gratitude.

The Grass is Actually Greener

I think the reason we don't see God in our lives is because we aren't really looking for God. We're looking for God's absence, not God's presence. Why would I say that? Because you'll always find what you're looking for. If you look into a relationship trying to find problems, you're going to find problems. If you look into a relationship trying to find happiness, you're going to find happiness. Are both present? Of course, but whichever one you are looking for is what you're going to find.

The Bible is scoured with wisdom that tells us nature is reflecting God to us. In fact, the Apostle Paul says in multiple writings that God is in and through all things.[2] Ready for me to reveal another secret of mine again? I sometimes find and connect with God better while I'm alone in nature than I do with others at church. I don't think it's one or the other, I think both are necessary. I think it's necessary for me to connect with God alone, and I think it's necessary for me to connect to God with others. Both are essential, and they serve different purposes. When I connect with God alone, particularly in nature, I have an ethereal, divine experience with God. It helps me see God as a Creator or Source. When I connect to God with others, I have an approachable, relatable experience with God. It helps me see God as a Father or Friend. I need both for a healthy perspective and encounter with the Almighty.

I love walking or running on the beach at sunrise and sunset. It's my favorite place and my favorite time. I find it incredibly easy to connect with God during those times. It offers me a transcendent experience and perspective from God on life. I see the sunrise and am immediately mesmerized by the beautiful imagination God must have to have set that into motion. I then begin to think about how the solar system works and how I'm a small speck on this planet

---

[2] Colossians 1:16-17, Ephesians 1:22, Ephesians 4:6, etc.

called Earth in this solar system in a galaxy called the Milky Way. Then I begin to think about how many millions of galaxies there are and why a God who is the Source of it all would take an interest in the life of one species on one planet in one solar system in one of these millions of galaxies, and who even knows how far that could stretch? What if galaxies are small pieces of something even larger? And if I follow Jesus, who I believe to be the heart of God, was he only sent to Earth? Is there another species of God's heart in another galaxy somewhere? You see, it's pretty dangerous for me to begin asking questions, because they get really big really fast. But I don't have to know the answer, and God's bigger than any question I can come up with, so it's all good. It really just draws me into wanting to live with more intention, because I am inspired by creation to reflect God to humanity.

  I don't know where you see shades of God in nature. Maybe it's the way the flowers bloom, or the way bees pollinate, or the way birds build nests, or the silence of the desert, or the mystery of the northern lights, or the canyons, the oceans, waterfalls, or trees. Maybe it's the cloud formations, or the view from a plane, the images from space, the depths of the sea, the animals in the wild, or the fingerprint of a newborn. But there are countless features in nature that showcase the character of God. We are shown glimpses of who God is through every molecule in nature, and we can see God in every square inch if we're looking for Him. The grass is actually greener if you can see God's presence in its design and function. The sky is actually bluer if you can discover the presence of God through its palette. Humanity is actually breathtaking if you will discover the image of God in every person. If you can't see it, you aren't looking for it.

Being in nature and catching glimpses of God brings belonging into perspective for me. I am a human, a species on Earth. I am a piece of nature's puzzle. My existence is from the imagination of God. As a human, I innately belong. Not because of anything other than my humanity. God designed humanity to belong, and even if you don't believe you belong, you still belong, because you can't stop being human. Knowing I belong in a grander scheme than what I can learn or obtain or experience in life is transcending to my culture. As a human, my beliefs are as relative as the humans I encounter. Literally. Everything is learned. My belonging transcends those beliefs, because I belong to the One who designed me. I belong to the One who is responsible for my existence. I belong to the One who passionately expresses through all of nature that I belong. I am human, crafted in the image of God, and I belong.

FIVE
COMMUNITY & IDENTITY

Humans have this intrinsic need in the deep core of their being to belong. It's as if our individual identity is somehow wrapped up in our communal belonging. It's interesting, because as we talked about in the last chapter, humanity is crafted in the image of God. I think this need to belong is divinely genetic, as we understand God to be a communal Being. In the first chapter of the Bible we read that God refers to Himself in the plural form, as if to insinuate community.

> *Then God said, 'Let us make mankind in our image, in our likeness.'*
> **Genesis 1:26**

Allow me to interject.

> *Then God [singular] said, 'Let us [plural] make mankind in our [plural] image, in our [plural] likeness.'*
> **Genesis 1:26**

It's as if there are multiple expressions of a single God. Most Christians would use this to point to the Trinity or a triune Godhead. For our purposes, I want to draw a more relatable conclusion that God is a community all by Himself. Since humanity is crafted in God's image, the need for belonging comes from God since God is a divine community. The difference is that unlike God, who is Himself a community, we need other humans to form a community, which makes belonging a core desire of humanity.

Individualism

One of the focal points of Christianity is our personal relationship with God. It's the idea that my destiny is contingent upon my personal interaction with God through the course of my life. I certainly value a personal relationship with God, but not to the extent that I was taught about the principle. I think we have failed to differentiate a personal relationship - or what I would call a personal faith journey - from faith-based individualism. I was taught individualism, where my walk with God was all about my personal development and my personal growth in the faith. When I read the Bible, I see a more community-centered faith, which makes sense since God is a community. I would argue that it's not either one or the other; rather it's both at the same time.

My journey with God is only as personal as it is communal. In fact, I propose that everyone has a communal journey with God, and we have the option to also make it a personal journey with God. God is above all and in all and through all; therefore, our communal relationship with God is default, because it's not contingent on the individual. However, a personal journey with God is only as the individual pursues it. God is the Source of all humanity, and our communal journey with God is what connects all of us as humans. God shines light on us all, sends rain on us all, gives breath to us all, extends love and mercy and kindness and forgiveness to us all, and pursues us all with the vital gift of life. God's pursuit of us through these necessities and more is what establishes and sustains humanity's communal relationship with God. If you're alive, you're in a relationship with God, because God is giving you breath, and you're receiving it and giving it back. It's a relationship that's as personal as it is communal.

Individualism is dangerous to our empathy toward humanity, because we think we no longer share a common relationship to God with the rest of humanity, but only with those who believe like us.

Individualism creates distance, fear, and exclusion. Individualism is what empowers religious hate, bigotry, racism, sexism, oppression, and eliteness. At some point we have to understand as humans that we are all in this together - not just the people in our denomination or the people in our country or the people in our religion - all of us, all of humanity is in this together. We are all living on the same planet, breathing the same air, crafted in the image of the same God. We belong to each other, we belong to God, and we are a default community bonded by the love of God.

Community

Between the words of Jesus in Matthew 22[3], when he's referring to the greatest commandment, and the words of John in 1 John 4[4], we can see that to love God is to love your neighbor as yourself. I think it's pretty easy to make the argument that you have to love yourself well in order to love your neighbor well, and you have to love your neighbor well in order to love

---

[3] "Teacher, which command in the law is the greatest?" He said to him, "Love the Lord your God with all your heart, with all your soul, and with all your mind. This is the greatest and most important command. The second is like it: Love your neighbor as yourself. All the Law and the Prophets depend on these two commands." Matthew 22:36-40.

[4] Dear friends, let us love one another, because love is from God, and everyone who loves has been born of God and knows God. The one who does not love does not know God, because God is love. 1 John 4:7-8.

God well. I would even say that loving your neighbor as yourself is the act of loving God. It takes a community to love God well.

We often strip ourselves away from the group when we think about God in a relationship with us, but God's relationship with us is only made possible by God's relationship with the community of humanity. What I'm saying is that I think we over-personalize what God intended to be all-encompassing. When we over-personalize the Bible, or what we believe about God, or what we believe about life, it makes exclusion a natural tendency. When we universalize the Bible, or God, or life, it makes inclusion a natural tendency. The truth is God doesn't just love me or only humans like me who also believe like me. God loves humanity; and because God loves humanity, God loves me.

There is this innate love that parents have for their children. I remember when our first daughter, Andie, was born in November of 2011. We had gone through two miscarriages the year prior, and we were so nervous about her arrival. I was completely out of character during the whole experience. I was off reading the newspaper while Andrea was walking around the hospital with her mom and sister attempting to induce labor. I never read the newspaper, ever. But don't worry, I also had hospital sushi while reading the newspaper. You can imagine the formaldehyde smell and taste of sushi made in a hospital cafeteria in Winchester, Virginia. But there I was, wrist deep in sushi, reading the newspaper, living my best life. Once we got into the delivery room, it was time for the epidural. I don't do needles or blood or anything of the sort. Especially when my wife is involved. I had no idea what was going to happen, but had I only known, it would've gone differently. The anesthesiologist brought in his cart of supplies and pulled out a seemingly six-foot needle that was supposedly going to go between two of my wife's vertebrae. He then read a clause and asked us to sign and verbally agree that we understand this could result in paralysis and death, and neither he nor the hospital could be held responsible. Then he began to administer the epidural. I know I should have been holding Andrea's hand and talking her through this scary moment, but I was hunkered over and hyperventilating in a chair in the corner with my head hung between my knees, rocking back and forth.

Needless to say, I was never allowed in the room again during the epidurals for the births of our younger two girls, Aisley and Avie.

When Andie was finally delivered, I remember holding her in my hands, tears in my eyes, kissing my wife. We smiled, we laughed, we cried, and we held each other close. There was a deep love that was so natural and undeniable that we shared together for this beautiful newborn girl who looked just like the both of us, made in our image. I think that's how it is for God and humanity, who is made in His image. But I think God's love for humanity is on an unfathomable level and depth that we could never begin to approach with thoughts or words or understanding. It can only be received, not understood, nor reciprocated.

When Andrea and I were talking about having Aisley, our middle daughter - or as Andrea refers to her: our *centerpiece* - we feared not being able to love her as much as we loved Andie. We couldn't imagine having another love that could be as deep. But along came Aisley, and the depth of love for her was naturally immediate once again. And then came Avie. Once again, we loved her just as deeply, just as quickly, just as naturally. We could never possibly love any of our girls more than the other. They each have our deepest love that is unconditional and intrinsic. We love them, we would give ourselves for them, and there's nothing they could ever do to stop us from loving them. They're our children, made in our image.

When we realize God's unconditional and intrinsic love for humanity, it transforms the way we see and interact with humanity. We would no longer attempt to convert other humans to our way of interacting with God; rather, we would invite them to participate in our interaction with God while also participating in their interaction with God. God becomes community-centered when we open our eyes to the beautiful truth of who God is. God is love, and His dwelling place is within humanity.

Some of the byproducts of this realization are empathy, compassion, love, and participation. We naturally become like Jesus and reflect the character of God when we embrace the community of humanity with God. It makes the world better, it makes life better, and it makes us better.

Identity

I don't know if it's always been this way, but in my lifetime humans seem to go on a quest to find themselves sometime after high school. This is more of an existential journey that connects one's self to one's identity. This journey often begins with questions like:

Who am I?

Why am I here?

What is my purpose?

Where do I belong?

The timing of these journeys is ironic, since most journeymen have just completed an eighteen year intensive of being taught who they were supposed to be - or who others wanted them to be. We call it upbringing and education. After years have been spent shaping the lives of these journeymen, they decide to forsake all they know in search of who they are and where they belong. It's really a beautiful journey to be honest, and more people would do it if they could fund it. Nevertheless, it's a journey they could have been having all along if the communities of their upbringing and education would have valued discovery and diversity over regulation and information, creating a space to thrive in belonging as a unique piece of the whole.

It's like a microchip in a computer. The chip is unique, with a different function from the screen, keys, and drive. It's uniqueness, however, is only as valuable as it is related to the community of parts that make up the computer. The chip has to have a place to belong in order to be unique, because it was never created to function on its own. But when the chip, the screen, the keys, the drive, and all the other unique parts are placed in community with each other, they serve a purpose as an individual that's only as great as the sum of all the parts working together. In a community, it's a computer; individually, it's a microchip. The identity is based on having a place to belong.

When I recognize that I am a unique individual, created in the image of God to serve a unique purpose, it's only when I find a place to belong in the community of humanity that my purpose now functions. Individually, I am Aaron; in a community, I am father, husband, teacher, brother, friend. Identity is always tied to our belonging.

Deconstruction

It's often confusing and frustrating for a parent, pastor, or teacher to watch a person they've poured into and formed break free to go reinvent who they are, essentially undoing all of the formative work accomplished in their life. It can feel like a slap in the face, I imagine; I'm not really sure, I've only been on the other end of it.

I wonder if that frustration isn't rooted in fear and somehow also self-inflicted? I believe it's both. We often have the tendency to recreate what we know in others. For instance, if we believe and adhere to a systematic theology, we instill those principles into our kids, parishioners, and students. We push them through a process of disciplines in order to grow them into who we believe God wants them to be. When those kids, parishioners, and students decide they want to have their own faith journey that is about discovery and transformation rather than disciplines and information, the natural tendency of the parents, pastors, and teachers is to attempt to convince them otherwise and eventually write them off out of frustration and confusion.

It's self-inflicted, because we are trying to shape them into our own image of God. In doing so, we may mean well, but we set ourselves up for deep hurt and frustration when they want to pursue God's image in them rather than our image of God. It's also rooted in fear, because we fear what we can't control and don't understand that has the possibility to end in contradiction of who we are and what we believe. We may not say it, but deep down we believe we have the corner on God, so much so that we fear the fate of others who don't believe the way we believe. After all, would we follow God with such vigor and teach others to follow Him too if we weren't convinced our beliefs and convictions were accurate? It's a natural human tendency that leads us to exclusion and self rather than inclusion and community - and remember, God is community.

The deconstruction of the beliefs and traditions we've been taught isn't a dangerous journey; it's a necessary journey that leads one to discover who she really is, how God interacts with her, and what God can do through her. The point of deconstruction is not to aimlessly tear apart a traditional belief system out of spite or bitterness, but to address apparent issues and inner struggles with thoughtful questions and open-minded reflection and prayer. Similar to what we discussed in chapter three, true deconstruction is seeking wisdom, not answers. The end goal is not a reconstruction of a hybrid or new faith. The goal is a discovery of God, self, and purpose.

It's not a moment. It's not a phase. It's a journey. The journey of faith is less about what we are supposed to believe and more about who we were meant to be. It's about community and identity, and when we discover God for ourselves, we always find belonging in Him.

Aaron Brewer

SIX
PAIN & PASSION

It's hard to talk about identity, like we did in the last chapter, and not talk about our past and our pain. It's often our past and our pain, or even the pains of our past, that have birthed our present identity. I know from the chapter title that you think we're going to talk about pain and passion, but that's not really what this chapter is about at its deepest core. Sure, we're going to talk about those things, but those are subsequent to the main subject of this chapter: purpose. So why the confusing title? Because the secret to your purpose lives in the intersection of your pain and your passion.

The big question for teens who are Jesus followers is, "What is God's will for my life?" They want to know their purpose, and they want their life to matter. I remember asking this question as a teenager and searching for the answer. I would read the Bible looking for it. I would pray and ask God to show me a clear sign as to what my purpose was meant to be. Although I believe my life has a specific purpose, I can't say there was a voice from heaven that spoke to me and gave me the direction for my life. There was no big event that occurred that set the course of my life's purpose. There was no voice that prophetically spoke over my life and said that God would do a specific purpose through me. Yet I still discovered and pursued the purpose God had for my life. It seemed to be birthed from the desires God designed into my personality.

Are you curious about your purpose and how to zoom in on it? I think there's a straightforward way to discover it, so let's talk about it!

Pain

Here's a question that's not so fun to answer or think about, but what is the greatest place of pain in your story? When you are asked to tell your life story, what are the major events that caused you pain that you would talk about? For most of us, those events or seasons are vivid. After all, they helped shape us into who we are and how we think today, for better or for worse.

I know pains are personal, and I know pains are tragic.

We often view the pains in our past as something to get over or get past in order to find healing. We convince ourselves we can be someone great and accomplish something significant despite our pain. I like to flip it and think that we can be someone great and accomplish something significant because of our pain.

It's okay to still remember the past, and it's okay for the past to still sting - it was a painful piece of your story. But your painful past doesn't get to be a towering demon casting shade over your future. It doesn't get to hold the pen to your next chapter. Jesus is not just the author and finisher of your faith, but He is the author and finisher of your story too.

Pain is tricky, because it gives us a false lens to view life through. The lens of pain distorts our view of God, others and self. We begin to ask:

Why did God cause this to happen?

Why did God allow this to happen?

How could that person do that to me?

Am I really a terrible person?

Am I unlovable?

Our natural response to pain is to point blame. We point the blame at others, ourselves and God. Are others to blame? Maybe, but we're all human, and we all have the same sin and need the same savior. Are we to blame? Maybe, but we're all human, and we all have the same sin and need the same savior. Is God to blame? Well, He's not human, He is the antithesis of sin, and He is the savior. So, no, God can't be the blame. But maybe we're not asking the right question. Maybe our natural response of pointing blame isn't the appropriate response at all. Perhaps the appropriate response to pain is opportunity. Perhaps the right questions to ask are something like:

God, can you take my brokenness and piece me back together into something more beautiful?

God, will you take my pain and give it a purpose beyond its past?

God, can you use my story to transform someone else's life?

I don't believe God causes or allows bad things to happen, but I do believe that when those things happen, God can take what was meant for evil and use it for good in our lives and in the lives of others. I believe God can give every pain a new purpose to serve our future. And when we begin to ask the right questions, we replace the false lens of pain with the true lens of opportunity.

Our painful past can only imprison us with our permission. But God has given us His Spirit, and where the Spirit of the Lord is there is freedom. So let freedom ring over the painful past of your story, and let the future God has for you be poised with your pain in hand repurposed for His glory.

Passion

You know that thing that you've always wanted to do, or who you've always wanted to be? You know what I'm talking about - it's that dream you've always had or that prompting that you have felt in your spirit that perhaps God could use you to make a difference in a certain way. Maybe you would define it as your passion. That's how I'm going to define it right now.

For most of us, it's always just a little bit beyond our reach, a little bit beyond our comfort zone, a little bit beyond our current ability, and a little bit beyond our current resources. We've allowed the hesitation of fear, the thought of uncertainty, and the familiarity of comfort keep us just far enough away from the edge to never leap in faith toward the dream of our destiny. But I think the very things that are keeping us from pursuing our passion are the very things that God wants to use to accomplish our passion.

It's just a little bit beyond *our* reach. It's just a little bit beyond *our* comfort zone. It's just a little bit beyond *our* ability. It's just a little bit beyond *our* resources. We can't accomplish our passion, our dream, our purpose within our own reach, comfort, ability, and resources. But it is within *God's* reach, and it is within *God's* comfort zone, and it is within *God's* ability, and it is within *God's* resources. We were never built to be strong enough or smart enough or just plain enough. It is through our weakness that His strength is made perfect. What we can accomplish through our own ability is limited, but with God, we get to accomplish our calling through His limitless ability, strength, and resources.

God has given you talent and desire, and He has wired you with a unique personality. He created you to have everything that you need in order to leap beyond your ability and resources and circumstances into the future and purpose that He has called you to in order to make a difference in the world. The struggle is to actually take the leap of faith, which very few of us ever do; but the One who has called you will be faithful to sustain you!

I'm convinced that the reason most of us never see the mighty hand of God in our lives is because God has never had to come through for us. We never put ourselves in a situation so far out of our own control that God gets to step in and do His work. I think that's why our passion is just beyond our control - so we can see and know that it is God working for us, in us, and through us. Pushing through our own uncertainty allows us to discover the absolute certainty of God's purpose for us.

The Big Move

I told you that Andrea and I started a church in our hometown of Winchester, Virginia. Within two years there were several hundred people that would call our church home, and our family was thriving at home and work. About halfway through 2020, Andrea and I felt the prompting of God to enter a new season of life and ministry. We didn't know exactly what that looked like, but we knew from experience that we had to take a leap of faith. We transitioned the church to new leaders who we developed and love, and we moved to the Crystal Coast of North Carolina.

Sounds seamless, right? It was anything but seamless.

We put our house on the market in Virginia, and it sold within three days. We found a home right on the beach that we adored. The sellers wouldn't come off of the price, so we entered a contract at the very peak of our affordability.

We came to the beach for vacation in August with Andrea's family on the very island we were moving to. We were so excited to lay eyes on our new home for the very first time. As we walked through the two-bedroom condo with our realtor, we quickly came to realize that the pictures online were extremely enhanced. The ceiling was cracked from shifting, every wall and baseboard were beaten from rental traffic, all of the exterior windows were allowing moisture through the seams - causing the trim to warp, and there was mold in the ceiling. The list goes on, but I think you get the point.

Our only saving grace was looking out the front windows and seeing the waves crash along the shore. It was a beautiful sight and a lovely sound that we knew would never get old. But were we willing to overlook all of the problems and the hefty price tag for the view?

It turns out that in North Carolina you can back out of a contract as a buyer for no reason at all. So that's what we did, and we continued to look for other homes on the island. We found a beautiful little bungalow that had just been renovated to look like a coastal dream. It also had an extra bedroom and a fantastic yard space for entertaining! With three girls, we needed the third room. We took off the next morning to meet our realtor at the bungalow, and on our way there, she called to tell us an offer was accepted a few minutes earlier and the house was no longer on the market.

Filled with disappointment, we began looking for other options, and nothing was turning up. Everything was either unaffordable or in terrible shape.

To make things worse, that afternoon we got a call from our lender. The bank asked me to have our church provide a statement that we would continue to receive our income for at least three more years. I had to relay to our lender that I had quit my job and would not be receiving that income at all. As you might be guessing, they began to inform me that we would no longer be approved for a loan of any amount.

We were confused and devastated. We started praying and questioning God, because we really felt in our hearts that He was prompting us to make this move and begin this new ministry and season. Could we be completely mistaken?

You Don't Have To Believe To Belong

The lender told me that if I could find a cosigner for the loan, I might still be approved. That was no problem, because we knew my parents would cosign for us, and they are very successful business owners in our hometown. I picked up the phone and called my dad, told him the situation and asked him to cosign. He told me that he would talk to my mom and call me back. He didn't call back that day, which I knew was odd. He returned my phone call the next morning and, with a shaky voice, proceeded to tell me that after praying about it they just didn't feel comfortable cosigning for us.

At this point we were thoroughly shaken, hopeless, and helpless. I began showing Andrea unlivable places that our family could make a home, knowing this is not at all what we pictured when saying yes to God.

You know it was bad when I was saying things like, "This one doesn't have a roof, but we really like the sunshine, so we could make it work." Andrea didn't see the humor, but I was half serious. She was in tears, wondering how we were going to provide food and shelter for our three girls. You have to remember that we were leaving a life of extreme comfort and ease, not to mention that we were still on vacation with her family, trying to keep it all together.

I called a friend who is in the real estate industry, and he told me that I had three options: a nontraditional lender, hard money, or renting. A nontraditional lender can typically be creative with self-employed borrowers. Hard money is when you receive the large lump sum that you are borrowing, and the loan is due in three to five years with extremely high interest - just enough time to establish the history to get a traditional loan. Renting would also buy us the time to establish the history to get a traditional loan.

The only option I liked was the nontraditional lender, so I searched and called one in North Carolina. His name was Lloyd. Lloyd heard our story and told us that no one in the state is going to lend us any money whatsoever, but he wished us the best of luck. That was the last glimmer of hope we had, and our light had been snuffed completely out. We felt like there were no more options, we had mistaken God's voice, and we had thrown our lives away.

We prayed and wept together. Andrea's unshakable faith caused her to continue looking at listings online. She showed me a listing that caught her attention but was visually bleak. It was a sound-front condo in the very center of the island, across the street from the ocean, and it had been on the market for about a year. The pictures were awkwardly angled, dark and messy, as if they were taken on an old flip phone. The description was unlike any other description I had ever read. It was lengthy and wordy, almost like a journal entry of one's jumbled thoughts. The very bottom of the description said to call Bill Wiggins if interested and listed three or four different numbers where he could be reached if he didn't pick up at one of the others. Seriously.

I called the first number, and an elderly, distinguished voice answered, "Bill Wiggins."

Me: "Hi, my name is Aaron Brewer, and my wife and I are looking at your condo online. Have you sold it yet?"

Bill: "Um, no, I haven't."

Me: "Ok. Can we see it?"

Bill: "Sure."

Click! He was gone. Just like that. I thought, "What in the world? No wonder this place is still on the market! I should've known not to call that number."

Two minutes later my phone rings.

Me: "Hello?"

Bill: "Aaron, this is Bill Wiggins. Has my brother called you?"

Me: "No."

Bill: "Ok, he will."

Click! He's gone again. No joke!

Two minutes later my phone rings again.

Me: "Hello?"

Bill: "Aaron, this is Bill Wiggins. Has my brother called you?"

Me: "No."

Bill: "Ok, he will."

Click!

Two minutes later my phone rings yet again.

Me: "Hello?"

This time, an elderly, tinny voice with a country twang responded, "Baron? This is Robert Wiggins, Bill's brother." Legit, he called me Baron!

Me: "Yes, this is Aaron."

Robert: "I'm sorry for callin' ya Baron, Aaron. Look, meet me over at the condo in one hour."

So Andrea and I drove down the island to meet Robert at Bill's condo. There was an exquisite outdoor pool with fountains in front of the facility, and there was covered parking under the condominiums. We greeted Robert and went into the elevator up to his brother's condo. The elevator opened to a beautiful and spacious common area overlooking the ocean. We approached the unit, which had a deep front porch with an ocean view. There was a small hand written note taped to the front door that said,

"FOR SALE. CALL BILL WIGGINS."

Robert opened the front door, and once again, the inside of the home did not match the pictures online. But this time, in the very best of ways.

The entryway had ceramic tile, as did the kitchen, laundry room and all the bathrooms. We noticed a glue-like smell as soon as we walked through the front door. It was the smell of brand new carpet, which ran down the hallway, in each bedroom, and in the living room. All three bedrooms were suites with their own large bathrooms. We noticed crown molding throughout the entire house, along with tray ceilings in each bedroom. The kitchen had high-end appliances, granite countertops and a breakfast bar. The master bedroom had a huge bathroom with a walk-in closet, soaking jacuzzi tub and walk-in shower. There was a balcony that was the same spacious depth as the front porch, accessible through both the living room and the master bedroom, giving both rooms a spectacular panoramic view. It overlooked Bogue Sound and ran the entire length of the condo. From the balcony, we noticed that the facility had a pier, floating dock, beach, watercraft storage, and a boat ramp into the sound. The condominium was built with concrete and steel and was designed to be "hurricane-proof." There was a perplexing situation that we noticed after walking through the condo: everything seemed to be unused. And this is when we heard the story of Bill Wiggins from his brother, Robert.

Bill had moved into the condo as a retirement home in 2016. He lived in it for two weeks before he had to relocate to Virginia Beach for assisted living, and he never rented this condo in case he ever returned. The facility he was now residing in happened to be a Westminster Canterbury, which also happened to have a location in Winchester, Virginia, where my grandmother was formerly a nurse. This was an interesting connection between Bill and us. We also found out from Robert that Bill had made a fortune in the real estate business in Woodbridge, Virginia, which was just a short distance from our hometown.

After visiting and admiring the condo, we headed toward the front door. Robert ushered us back onto the elevator and pushed a button. However, the elevator went up instead of down, and a voice came on the elevator and said, "Penthouse." Andrea and I were standing behind Robert and looked at each other with jaws dropped. The elevator door opened, and we began to wander around the top level of this incredible high-rise. The views alone were breathtaking, but we couldn't believe what we were experiencing. The penthouse had a game room with billiards, ping pong, shuffleboard and more, overlooking the ocean. There was a full fitness center overlooking the ocean. There was a large event room with a banquet kitchen and serving bar overlooking the sound. There was a study with modern coastal decor and furniture, hundreds of books, including Bible and theology resources, all overlooking the sound. There was even an outdoor viewing deck around the penthouse, perfect for viewing the watercolor sunsets. *Where in the world were we, and how did we get here?*

We knew in the back of our minds as incredible as this place was that we still had a major problem. We couldn't get a loan. But this place felt so perfect; it felt like home. While Robert was showing us around the condo and the penthouse, he was asking us about our family and jobs. I told him we were ministers and were relocating to the Crystal Coast. He said, "Call Bill, he'll work with ya!" We thought that was a little strange but didn't think much of it. That is, until he said it three more times: "Call Bill, he'll work with ya!" Finally after stepping out of the elevator on our way out, Andrea looked at me and said, "Would you just call Bill so we don't have to hear him say that again?"

I walked out onto the pier to call Bill - after all, apparently he'd work with us - and Andrea walked over to Robert's car to meet his wife, Cathy, and his dog, Trucker.

Bill: "Bill Wiggins."

Me: "Hey, Bill. It's Aaron. We just walked through the condo with your brother."

Bill: "Did you like it?"

Me: "Oh, yes, it's fabulous!"

Bill: "Well, do you want it?"

Me: (Not dare mentioning we couldn't get approved for a loan,) "Well, we really like it."

Bill: "I assume you want the owner financing."

Me: "Say that again?"

Bill: "I assume you want the owner financing. You don't want to have to go to the bank."

Me: "No, sir, I don't want to go to the bank!"

Bill: "Okay, great. How about 4% at a 30-year rate for 10 years? And since you have a young family, don't worry about the principle, just pay the interest. And then if you ever have any extra, just put it toward the principle - no early payoff penalty!"

Me: "I'm sorry, can you say all of that just one more time?"

And sure enough, I had heard every detail correctly. I hung up the phone and was in a daze of amazement at what had just taken place. I took off running up the pier toward Andrea who was in the car garage still talking to Robert and Cathy. As I approached them, I heard Andrea saying, "Sister Cathy *this*," and "Sister Cathy *that*." I was thinking, "What's going on here?" When Robert and Andrea had informed Cathy that we were ministers, she took right to Andrea and had already invited us over to their home for dinner by the time I got back from the phone!

We got in the car, and I informed Andrea about the phone call with Bill. We wept and prayed again, this time in thanks to God. We pondered on the car ride back to the vacation house about the irony and provision of God. Everything we tried to control fell apart: the house, the loan, the timing, etc., but God's plan was far beyond our wildest dreams and expectations. He already had it all in place just waiting for us - for quite some time! God provided a home, the financing, a family, and food.

But God doesn't just supply all of our needs according to *our* riches; He supplies all of our needs according to *His* riches. Yep, the story gets even better.

We arrived at the beach house to inform Andrea's parents about the great news. They told us that they had felt prompted to pray with Andrea's grandmother about this particular place while we were headed out, because they just felt God was up to something. And sure enough, He was! We couldn't wait to show Andrea's family the home God was providing, so I called Robert. He agreed to meet us back at the condo.

As Andrea was showing her family around the place, my father-in-law, Darrell, was sitting and chatting with Robert at a round outdoor table that Bill had left in the living room.

Darrell: "Robert, do you live around here?"

Robert: "Yep, lived here all my life. I live right across the water on the riverside of Morehead City."

Darrell: "Do you spend much time on the water?"

Robert: "Yeah, I love the water. I got a new boat with a brand new engine on it, but I don't like to go out by myself because of my age, and I ain't got nobody to go with me."

I immediately swung around in awe and excitement with my hand raised in the air, "Robert, pick me! I'll go with you!" (And at the time of writing this,

Robert and I have gone fishing on the ocean almost every week together since our move to North Carolina.)

I told Andrea what had just transpired, and she said almost with a chuckle, "At this point, the only thing God hasn't given us is a kayak." On our way out the door, Robert said to us, "Oh, by the way, I have a couple kayaks if y'all ever wanna borrow 'em." No joke! You can't make this stuff up.

But not only does God supply our needs according to His riches, but He also supplies others' needs through His supply of ours.

We were about two weeks away from closing on our home in Virginia when we got a call from our realtor. She said that the family buying our home ran into some financial trouble and could no longer make the purchase. We had to put our house back on the market. Just after everything was looking so fantastic, it all fell apart again - or so it seemed.

Our house sold in three days once again, and every time it showed we would pray, "God, may whoever walks through these doors experience You while in our home." We received a contract from a family in northern Virginia, and a few weeks later we signed the papers and packed our moving truck. This house was in our hometown. We had built it and lived in it for ten years. It had seen the best and worst parts of our lives. It was the place where we mourned two miscarriages. It was the place where we brought all three of our girls home from the hospital. It was the place we poured our love into, and it had kept us safe and secure for a decade. Before we drove away for the last time, Andrea led us in an emotional prayer in the front yard. She prayed that the new owners, whoever they were, would experience the love of God while living in the home, and that God would bless their family through our home. We pulled out of the driveway and drove to Bogue Banks, our little island on the Crystal Coast of North Carolina we would soon call home.

A few weeks later, Andrea received a message from our old neighbor in Virginia. She told Andrea she was surprised to find out the occupation of the new owners of our old home, and she thought we just needed to know. they were pastors who led a multi-site church with two locations, one in northern Virginia and one in central Virginia. Our neighborhood was situated between the two campuses and was in perfect placement for them to live in order to pastor their churches effectively and intimately.

God didn't just supply our needs according to His riches, but He also supplied the needs of others who were pursuing their calling, and He did it through our leap of faith.

Just Leap!

Our story is an incredible display of God's strength being made reality through our weakness. It's the perfect picture of God's timing, His provision, and His sustaining faithfulness when we leap beyond our own reach, comfort, ability, and resources toward the passion He has placed within us. Think about all of the crazy things that happened and how intricate God's design was. Had we received our loan and moved into either of the houses we had previously desired, we would've never seen God come through with His provision, because we would've come through with our provision - and we probably would've said, "Thanks for making a way, God." I wonder how many times we thank God for *our* best, but He wanted to give us *His* best? I wonder how many times we thank God for *our* ability, but He wanted to show us *His* ability?

Think about my parents. They had the resources and ability to cosign for us, but had they not prayed and listened to the voice of God, or if they had not had the hard conversation with us of denial, God wouldn't have had the opportunity to come through. I believe sometimes our obedience to God not only has the power to affect our own lives, but to affect the miracle in someone else's life too. I thank God for my parents who prayed before acting, and I thank God they obeyed His voice, no matter how difficult.

What if Bill had sold the unit during the last year or not had to go to Virginia Beach? What if Robert wouldn't have brought Cathy along? What if my father-in-law wouldn't have asked Robert about his life? What if everything would have gone as Andrea and I had hoped and planned? What if the original buyers of our home would have gone through with their purchase? What if Andrea's family hadn't prayed before we looked at the condo? What if Andrea hadn't led our family in prayer so many times over the showings and the new homeowners?

Everything that stands in the gap between you and your passion is out of your control, but it's all within God's reach and power. And the One who has called you will be faithful to sustain you.

Don't wait a day longer, decide in this moment - while reading these words - that you are going to take that leap. I'm here to tell you that God will blow your mind with His provision and plan. I know, because He did it for us.

Purpose

Did you forget we were talking about purpose after that story? That's right, this chapter isn't actually about pain or passion; it's about purpose. But you need both pain and passion in order to have purpose.

Purpose is something every human desires. We want to know that we belong, and we want to know that we are making a difference where we belong. We want to be a part of something bigger, we want to make a difference, and we want it to matter that we lived. How sad would it be if we gained all of the tangible things money could buy but never made a difference in the life of a single person? But a life lived in poverty that deeply impacted a countless number of people would be a life defined as meaningful and significant. What's the differentiator? Purpose. We all want it, we all need it, and so does the world we live in. That's what makes purpose stand apart. It has the power not only to change our own lives, but to transform the lives of others, leaving behind a significant spiritual footprint. Purpose gives us the ability to live well beyond our lifetime. There are facets of our lives today that are only so because of the impact of another person who lived decades, centuries, even millennia before. Something to keep in mind is that there are also facets of our lives today that we struggle through, not because of positive impact, but because of someone's negative impact on our world. The choices we make today will create the reality we experience tomorrow. So make them with purpose.

     Belonging and purpose go hand-in-hand. When we aren't living within the scope of our purpose, we often feel like we don't have a place to belong. We're like a fish out of water. When we are able to meet a need that otherwise would leave a void in our absence, we have found belonging. Our purpose creates a space for us to belong. It gives us a seat at the table of community.

     Perhaps the most difficult part of purpose is discovering it. How can I know that I have a specific purpose and what that purpose is? The good news is that you've already done the hard work, now you just have to put it all together.

If you were to draw two circles that slightly overlap, one would be labeled "pain" and the other "passion." Where they intersect or overlap would be labeled "purpose." Your purpose will always be found at the intersection of your greatest pain and your greatest passion. For me, one of my greatest pains came out of personal hurt and misdirection I received from spiritual leaders and teachers. Does it seem like that big of a deal now? Not as much, but it was the majority of my life during my formative years, so that hurt and manipulation molded me. Also for me, my greatest passion is communication, both written and spoken. Public speaking is my wheelhouse. So what's my purpose? Where does my pain and my passion intersect? I believe my purpose is to help others explore and expand their faith through my speaking and writing. I believe God has given me a unique message, presenting Him to humanity in a way that is powerful and practical.

That's an example of my purpose. Take the time to zoom in on the intersection of your pain and passion and discover your purpose.

Purpose isn't absolute. Your purpose can change from season to season - and that's okay. It's supposed to be that way. Your pains change, and you experience new pains. Your passions sometimes change too. Just keep living in that intersection to thrive in your purpose.

Wounds & Scars

There's something you need to know before we close out this chapter in order to protect yourself and protect others around you. Your purpose will be found from scars, not wounds. Never minister from your wounds; always minister from your scars.

When pain is fresh and we're still going through it, it's an open wound. When speaking from a place of pain, we say things we don't mean, we have a blurred vision of reality, and we get our mess all over everyone else. When we are speaking from scars and past pains, we have developed the wisdom and clarity that distance and healing have provided in order to help others through similar pains.

Something Andrea taught me was that hurting people hurt people, and healthy people heal people.

When you're hurting, you have the propensity to hurt people, intentionally and unintentionally. It's a natural self-defense mechanism. Healthy people not only heal people, but healthy people also realize when being hurt by someone else that it's not personal. That person just needs help healing. Not only do hurting people give hurt, they also receive it. Hurt becomes the filter hurting people experience life through. No matter how kind your gesture or how gentle your words, you will often offend a hurting person. It's not always how you did it or how you said it; it's how they received it.

Healthy words received through a hurting filter add salt to the wound. There are just some people who aren't ready to receive your ministry. Don't let it get you down, because there are millions of people who are, and God will bring them into your life when the time is ready.

The beauty of our journey is that God's purpose never wastes a pain in your past. God has a plan, you have a purpose, and you belong here to make a difference in the world.

Aaron Brewer

SEVEN
THEORY & THEOLOGY

My wife is currently homeschooling our two oldest girls. This is a first-time adventure for us all, and it's going surprisingly well. Andrea is the best mom in the world - seriously, she's probably way better than your mom. You know how you just wish that your child's elementary teacher knew your child's unique personality, interests, habits, struggles, and learning styles that make her unique? It's normal to think that no one would look after and care for your children like you would, and that's what we really want from others who are teaching our kids. And that's what makes Andrea a really good teacher for our girls. She gives grace to them in huge amounts and has incredible patience with them through the process, because she wants the very best for them in the most personal of ways. It's amazing to watch.

Andie was recently learning about the Lost Colony during her studies of the founding of America. The story has always fascinated me, and I've always thought I could go inspect the evidence and uncover what really happened to the colonists. During the last quarter of the sixteenth century, a large group of English families (over one hundred people) landed on Roanoke Island off the coast of North Carolina, where they had previously had conflict with Native Americans a few years prior when the English had first attempted to settle there. After establishing the colony, the English ships went back to their homeland to get some supplies for the new settlement. When they returned three years later, everything and everyone had vanished. There were no traces of what might have happened to their families, except for the word "CROATOAN" carved into a tree. History refers to this incident as the Lost Colony, and to this day it's still a mystery of what might have happened to the Roanoke Island settlers.

What do you think happened to the Lost Colony? Do you think they made friends with the Croatoan natives and colonized with them? Perhaps they were attacked by the unfriendly Wanchese tribe who were trying to protect their homeland? There are many theories on what might have happened to the colonists, but no one really knows for sure. It's still a mystery. Andie thinks that a hurricane may have formed in the Atlantic and wiped everything and everyone out. That's her theory.

Theory

I like theories. They often stretch my imagination. I really like theories that don't align with my vantage point, but give me an opportunity to see the world and people around me a little differently. It's fun (and beneficial) for me to put myself in someone else's shoes to see their perspective, their strength, their struggle, and their personality. Humanity would probably express much more empathy if we were all willing to put ourselves in the shoes of others.

Theories have the power to limit our freedom or expand our possibility. I wonder how many things in our lives are ruled by theories that may or may not be true. Perhaps we don't ever visit the beach or swim in the ocean, because we believe the theory that sharks are on the hunt for human blood. Perhaps we never apply for college, because we believe the theory that no one in our family is of collegiate caliber. Maybe we never take the risk of starting something new, because we believe the theory that we'll never make it. Maybe we never experience God through unexpected people and places, because we believe the theory that God only works a certain way and can only be found in a certain place. Or perhaps we always find an exhilarating adventure, because we believe the theory that life should be lived to the fullest. Perhaps we take advantage of every second with our loved ones, because we believe the theory that life is short and fragile. Maybe we see the hues of every painted sunset and hear the runs in every bird's song and discover the beauty in every small detail, because we believe the theory that we should live in every moment since we're not promised the next.

Theories impact our values, our fears, our actions, and our intentions. Theories can also define our belonging.

People often align themselves with a particular political party because of their theories on how a government should be run. People often align themselves with a particular denomination because of their theories on what they believe about God. No matter the context, when we choose to align our theories with the theories of others, we naturally find our belonging with them. Or so it seems. I would argue that we are mistaking alignment, agreement, and similarity with belonging. If our belonging is based on our common beliefs and theories, when our beliefs shift we no longer find belonging. But true belonging isn't based on alignment and similarity; true belonging offers us a seat at the table despite our beliefs, despite our mistakes, and despite our differences.

Theories can free you; and theories can confine you. I used to allow the theories I believed to confine me.

I met Andrea on summer break before my last semester of college. I was finishing my undergrad from a Southern Baptist university in Chattanooga, Tennessee, with a major in pastoral ministry. There were lots of theology classes that formed a solid systematic theology for me. When I graduated, I thought I knew everything about God and the Bible, and if anyone disagreed with me, they were wrong. Andrea didn't have a Baptist background. In fact, Andrea and her entire family graduated from a Pentecostal school that was the arch-rival of my university. Her parents were pastors of a large Pentecostal church in our hometown, and I soon found myself with the interesting choice of remaining Baptist or becoming Pentecostal. My grandfather was a Baptist preacher; my uncle was a Baptist preacher; my cousin was a Baptist preacher; and I went to school to be a Baptist preacher. All it took was one look at this Pentecostal preacher's daughter, and I was well on my way to running aisles and speaking in tongues!

It truly was a difficult season of transition for me to depart from my Baptist theology and embrace Pentecostal theology. Though they share some similarities, they also present some major differences. Along the way something profound happened within me that allowed me to eventually become the person I am today. I realized that my theories about God were actually confining me, not freeing me. I was a prisoner to a systematic theology, and I couldn't experience the outside world of possibility beyond the prison cell of my own theological mind. But to my amazement, when I let go of my confining theories about God, I found Him doing wonderful things beyond the limitations I had put on Him. I embraced a new theory that is now my only theological anchor, and I learned it from Andrea: God is unfigureoutable. It's the simplest, yet deepest truth you'll ever discover. And a few years later, I moved beyond my newfound Pentecostal theology to embrace what I call realized theology: living life to the fullest and experiencing God in every moment, in everything, and in everyone. And now my theories about God are no longer confining. My anchor theory that He is unfigureoutable is limitless and freeing, and I can now experience God outside of my own understanding.

In case you're wondering, Andrea arrived at this idea of realized theology long before I did, but was always patient and understanding of where my journey was leading me.

Theology

Theology isn't supposed to be a theory, theoretically. *See what I did there?* Theology, or the study of God, is deductive information about God directly from scripture. Over time, theologians have created systems of theology containing a set of beliefs and doctrines that people in agreement can adhere to.

Theory and theology are supposed to be different. But are they really?

Theology seems like it would be more factual since it's coming directly from scripture. For instance, you might read a direct statement about God in the Bible; therefore, you might assume it's a theological truth. Right? Maybe, maybe not. There are many direct statements attributed to God demanding the Old Testament Israelites to go take the land and leave no living thing in their path. I definitely would not form a theology around killing innocent people for land, nor would I actually attribute that concept to God. But there it is, all throughout the Old Testament. I think we have to keep in mind that the authors of the books in the Bible were human just like me and you. They wrote about their understanding of God, their interactions with God, and their theories about God. All of their writings were in the context of the culture they lived in, so it would make sense that they attributed their political success by way of mass killings to God's favor, because they lived in a barbaric culture where war was a way of life. It's not that God mandated their culture, but their culture was the lens through which they experienced God.

Every single book in the Bible was written by a human, yet every single book in the Bible was inspired by God. single book in the Bible shows us the theories, beliefs, and personalities of the authors and their experiences with God, written from their cultural perspectives. I don't find this to be problematic to theology, I find this to be exciting about theology. It means that our faith isn't something to be learned, but something to be experienced. It means that the authors wrote about their intimate interactions with God so that we could use it as faith to explore our own interactions with God. It means that the Word of God is alive and sharp, because it's still living through us today as we have our own experiences with God. We are a part of the story, and it is still unfolding through our lives.

So what do we do with the theology we've been taught? Well, that's a relative question based on who is reading my words. You were probably taught a different theology than I was. You might not believe in the Trinity, a literal seven day creation, or that foot-washing is a holy sacrament. But then again you might. There are many different Christian theologies that are believed and taught by people who really do love God with all their hearts. They may not all align, yet they each seem to have the full support of scriptural passages. Interesting, isn't it? So how can we know what is good theology and bad theology? Realize that it's all theory. There. I said it. Theology is really theory. It can be a correct theory or a false theory, but it's all really just a theory. There is always a circumstance that can happen outside of the box and understanding of our theology that leaves us scratching our heads. It can break our theology, or it can expand our theology. The best part about realizing that theology is a theory is that you get to make it transformative instead of informative. In other words, a theology learned is only a theory until it is experienced. Then it is a truth of Who God is to you. But be open-minded, because God made you uniquely, and He might show up in someone else's life in a totally different way. And that's okay, because He's unfigureoutable.

It's when we realize that we don't have the corner on God that we create a space of belonging for others to experience God alongside us. It also allows us to find belonging with others and experience God alongside them.

Aaron Brewer

EIGHT
FAITH & FEELINGS

Andrea and I were chatting one early fall morning on our balcony, which overlooks Bogue Sound. It was a warm, cloudless day on the Crystal Coast, and Andrea had another brilliant thought which became the inspiration for this chapter. She said, "We should always live *with* our feelings, but never *in* or *from* our feelings." My mind began to churn, and we preached to each other about the depth of this truth for a good half-hour.

I'm not a psychologist, and I don't administer counseling. It's way beyond my ability and pay grade. I have feelings, and I can handle them; but I don't know what to do with yours. You know what I mean? If you're in my presence and start crying, I'm immediately uncomfortable and will do or say anything to get out of dodge. I get it from my dad.

I never really saw my dad cry much while growing up. There was a moment of hysteria one time when I was eight years old. My mom was backing out of our driveway to take me to school, and my dad had already left for work but had forgotten something. As we were backing out of the driveway, he was pulling back into the driveway. He saw us, but Mom didn't see him. Dad thought he could swerve in around Mom before we backed out, and he ran into the back of us. They had a wreck - with each other - in our driveway. He was shedding some tears, and I don't think it was out of pain, though he was hyperbolically limping around in a panic. It was because he thought of all of the money it was going to cost to repair both cars, and he wasn't sure if their insurance would cover it since they wrecked into each other. And this was not the first time this had happened! Seriously.

Other than that wacky moment of hysteria, I had never really seen my dad shed tears until the day I left for college. My friend, Skippy, picked me up early one Friday morning to take me to the airport. I was going to be attending a one-year Bible school in Hudson, Florida, called Word of Life Bible Institute. As my dad hugged me goodbye, he didn't let go. His hands clenched the back of my shirt as he embraced me tightly, and he wept hard. That was a sobering moment for me to see the depth of love and feeling my dad had for me as I went off to school. I'll never forget it.

By the way, since then he's cried at our wedding, the birth of all three of our daughters, my brother's graduation, my brother's wedding, the death of his dog, the death of his dad, that time when his brother harassed me over lunch for my religious beliefs, when we moved to North Carolina, when his oldest brother died, and about every time something sappy happens. He's become more comfortable with his own feelings as he's aged; but he's never gotten more comfortable with anyone else's feelings.

If something is getting awkward, you'll look around, and he'll be gone. When we told my parents we were moving to the Crystal Coast, we were walking down the Old Town Walking Mall in Winchester, Virginia, to get some ice cream. We ended up getting ice cream with my mom, because my dad had vanished moments after we made the announcement, and Andrea and I didn't see him again until the next evening! That's how he handles the feelings of others, and so do I. We become MIA (missing in action). Andrea often jokes that in 2009 she started asking, "Where's Aaron?" and she hasn't stopped asking it since.

But as awkward as I am with feelings, I also understand and value their significance and importance to our thriving.

Feelings

Feelings aren't bad. Let me say that again, but this time read it slowly and let it sink in. Feelings aren't bad. You might feel depressed, you might feel angry, you might feel defeated, you might feel lonely, you might feel undervalued, you might feel any undesirable emotion, and that's okay. It's really okay. You're not defined by your feelings, and your feelings don't get to label you. They're just feelings. They are indicators of what is chemically and emotionally happening within your body and brain. And we should pay attention to our feelings and process our feelings, because feelings are indicators. But although feelings are great indicators, they are terrible instructors. They can tell you what's happening in you, but they should never tell you what's happening through you. You may feel depressed, but you don't have to end your life. You may feel angry, but you don't have to take someone else's life. You may feel undervalued, but you don't have to file for divorce. Your feelings don't get to control your actions; your faith does.

    Feelings were designed by God for our benefit. They're there for us to experience in their fullness. They help us navigate the extremities of life experiences. We would probably never ride the Tower of Terror at Disney World if there weren't a series of feelings that accompanied the experience. But we ride the insanity for the unfolding of fear, confusion, nostalgia, thrill, laughter, and rush of adrenaline. It's the series of vastly different and extreme feelings that keeps us filing in the long line to ride it just one more time. Life is the same way. We enjoy falling in love and having the feelings of excitement, wonder, and butterflies. We enjoy vacation and having the feelings of peace and clarity. On the other hand, we lament grieving the loss of a loved one and having the feelings of loss and emptiness. We despise being insulted because of the feelings of belittlement and insecurity. Feelings help us understand and navigate the experiences of life. They have a purpose, and they have a place; and they have the ability to hurt us instead of help us when we give them the wrong purpose and place.

It's normal for us to want to "feel all the feels." It's healthy to feel the feelings and allow them to run their full course. It's unhealthy, however, to allow the feelings you're experiencing to run *your* course. When we live life for the feeling and allow the feeling to live life for us, we become self-absorbed and live life with blinders on. We develop tunnel vision for our own desires and needs rather than focusing on the difference we can be making in the lives of those around us. When we live *in* our feelings, we lose the relationships around us, because we're only making emotional withdrawals from our loved ones and never any deposits. Eventually the emotional bank runs dry, and we're left all alone, all the while we were pursuing what we thought was fulfillment.

When we live in our feelings, we forfeit our belonging. It's not that others don't want us to be a part of their community; it's that we try to be our own community, because we live life aimlessly and selfishly, pursuing the moment.

In The Moment, Not For The Moment

Pepsi came out with a campaign in 2017 that was focused around the phrase, "Live For Now." It developed into a widely popular phrase in pop culture: live for the moment. The idea is that you live life for all the feelings the moment can offer. As you have figured out from your own life, feelings are always temporary, as is every moment. To live for something that's temporary is a terribly irresponsible way to live, and it will always leave you empty when that moment has ended.

I know it's just a phrase, but we tend to take simple phrases like this and adopt them as life mantras to live by. We actually frame our perspectives with these simple phrases that become filters our life is distorted through. And as you may know, a frame can showcase the picture, or a frame can detract from the picture. Your perspective has the power to change the interpretation of reality. Your perspective can make your life seem darker than it really is or brighter than it really is. It's all about how you frame it. Choose the phrases you frame your life with carefully.

When we live our lives chasing feelings and letting our feelings tell us where to go next, we are living for the moment.

Perhaps instead of living *for* the moment, we should live *in* the moment. After all, this moment is the only moment that really exists. Yesterday is gone, and tomorrow isn't here yet, so live in this moment with full intentionality. I believe God's will and purpose for us isn't always a big overarching theme, but rather a small task in this moment. We sometimes pursue the purpose of God through a vocation or big accomplishment. We think that God wants us to be a doctor, or a preacher, or a teacher, or a counselor, or whatever - that's His purpose for us. Maybe we view it as a big way to help humanity: starting a charity, opening an orphanage, reversing pollution. But what if we're approaching God's will and purpose backwards? What if God's purpose isn't what everyone else can see, what if it's what only we can see? What if it's not about the ribbon cutting ceremony at the orphanage, but it's about the small moments of empathy that compounded on one another that led up to this ceremony. We often pursue the championship trophy of God's purpose without showing up to the pre-season workouts. You can't have the championship trophy if you never compete in the championship game. You can't compete in the championship game if you never made it to the playoffs. You can't make it to the playoffs if you never win the regular season games. You can't win the regular season games if you never practice. And you can't practice if you didn't participate in the pre-season workouts.

God wants to accomplish the championship-trophy-purpose through your life, but realize that holding the championship trophy is just a moment that is made up of the smaller moments leading up to it.

Today's obedience will bring tomorrow's opportunities. Live *in* this moment, because there's a purpose God has for you in it. The next opportunity is directly related to your obedience in this moment. Don't live *for* the moment, because God has bigger moments for you. Live *in* this moment so that the bigger moments are made possible. God wants to do something magnificent through your life; all you have to do is live *in* this moment.

Faith

    Faith isn't the opposite of feelings, by any means. Faith recognizes feelings without allowing the feelings to rule reality. My feelings are real and my feelings may be deep, but my faith is bigger, and it rules over my feelings. When I may feel depressed, my faith recognizes my feelings but tells me the best is still yet to come. When I may feel angry, my faith recognizes my feelings but tells me to give grace and respond with kindness. My faith dictates my reality; my feelings surrender to my faith.

    Faith is tricky, isn't it? Growing up in the religion of Christianity, I always thought faith was synonymous with belief or trust. I thought if you had faith in Jesus, it meant you believed or trusted in Jesus. In general, faith is often synonymous with religious or spiritual beliefs and practice. It is portrayed to be equivalent with the religion one identifies with. We would ask, "What faith are you?" Colloquially, we tend to use the word *faith* in the same ways, but to do so dilutes the depth and beauty of its true meaning.

According to the biblical definition,

> *Now faith is the reality of what is hoped for, the proof of what is not seen.*
> **Romans 11:1**

So faith is not believing or hoping; faith is the physical reality of those things you spiritually hoped and believed. Faith is tangible. Faith is your now 2-year-old daughter when you prayed for years that God would bless you with a child when you couldn't conceive. Faith is your 9-to-5 job that you now work at when you were praying last year that God would provide. It's the tangible evidence of the very things you prayed and hoped for.

We often liken faith to the wind, but we get the illustration wrong. We say that the wind blows a tree over. You can't see the wind, but you see the power of it: that's faith. I would argue based on the biblical definition that faith is not represented by the wind; rather, faith is represented by the tree. Faith is not invisible; it's the visible evidence of the invisible God. Faith is the physical tree that was blown over, proving that the wind (God), which is invisible, really does exist and is showcasing its power as proof of its existence. So faith can be seen, and I would also argue that if we don't see faith, it's because we aren't looking for it.

Faith is the tangible evidence of the presence of God in our lives. When you look back on your life, where you undeniably see God's provision is faith itself. If you can't see God's provision when looking back, regardless of your story, it's not because it doesn't exist. It's because you aren't looking for it. The fact that you're able to read these words is proof of God's provision for your ability to comprehend a language, see with your eyes, and make non-verbal connections through the intelligence of your mind. That's a gift from God that not every human has. If you're reading these words, you are also breathing, and every breath is a gift from God. It's not that God hasn't provided; it's that you weren't looking for it.

Here's a reminder from chapter four that's also a universal truth to help diagnose your outlook on life. *You will always find what you're looking for.* If you start looking for problems in your marriage, you won't have to look far before you find a flaw in your communication, intimacy, or any other department of your relationship. But if you start looking for potential in your marriage, you won't have to look far before you find an opportunity in your communication, intimacy, or any other department of your relationship. You will always find what you're looking for. If you start looking for how imperfect your children are, you won't have to look far before you find all of their issues. But if you start looking for how wonderful your children are, you won't have to look far before you find all of their unique beauty. If you start looking for trouble at work, you're going to find it. But if you start looking for triumph at work, you're going to find it. You will always find what you're looking for.

So here's a question for you. *What parts of your life drag you down because of what you're looking for?* Here's another question. *What parts of your life could be spectacular by changing what you're looking for?* I don't know your answer to the first question, but I do know the answer to the second question: *All of them!* When you change your focus, you'll change your life.

When we choose to see God's presence in our lives, the things we are taking note of are the very molecules of faith. Those tangible moments give us hope for the future in spite of our feelings in the moment. If God came through before, He's going to come through again. He has a perfect track record, and He's not going to mess it up on our account. Our faith becomes hope that transcends our feelings. Our faith is always bigger than our feelings, because our faith is directly connected to our eternal God; and our feelings are directly connected to our temporary circumstances. Our feelings are valid and our feelings are real, but our feelings are not forecasting our future. Our faith gets to do that. Our faith sets the coordinates for the destination of our reality; while our feelings just indicate today's weather on our journey.

Faith Is Work

I don't want to paint the picture that faith removes the problems in life. Faith isn't a magical potion to set your life on a perfect track. Your problems still exist. Your marriage still takes work. Your mood still swings. Your kids still yell. Your bills still come every month. Your assignments are still due. Your feelings still hurt.

Faith isn't magical. Faith takes work. It's an intentional act of faith for you to think of a way to be grateful for that person and to choose to respond in kindness to the one whose words just cut you so deeply. It didn't come naturally, it wasn't an easy choice, and it didn't feel good; but it was an act of faith that took hard work. Faith sometimes hurts before it heals. It hurt to respond in kindness, but it made space for long term healing and acted as a vaccine to fend off bitterness and resentment. That's faith in action.

Faith plays the long game. It doesn't make momentary decisions that subside the pains of today at the expense of tomorrow. Faith makes deep, thoughtful, selfless choices that may hurt today in order to heal tomorrow. Faith does the right thing at the right time in the right way. And when you don't do the right thing at the right time in the right way, faith humbly admits the fault and asks for forgiveness. Faith allows you to be wrong so that the other person can be right. Faith forgives without requiring nor expecting an apology.

Faith isn't always fun, but it's always favorable. Faith takes work, but it's always rewarding.

It's not that the issues of life are no longer your issues, it's that faith gives you a lens to view the issues of life through hope and grace. The problems are still there, but now they're not dark clouds looming over you to stop you, they're stepping stones under you to help you. Your problems become opportunities when you approach them in faith.

When I was in middle school, I had an older friend in his sixties I went to church with named Joe Hepler. I'll never forget when Joe's life was radically changed by Jesus, and he became a completely different person. Joe was active and fun, always smiling and joking. Joe loved basketball, and he was pretty good at it. He would play with the teens and challenge them in one-on-one and shooting contests. Joe was tough to beat in a shooting contest, but he was even tougher to beat one-on-one. Not because Joe was quick or nimble, but because he was savage. Joe didn't care how old you were or how young you were, he was going to find a way to win, even if it meant throwing an elbow to the chest of a pre-teen boy so he could make that final basket. Every time I played against Joe, I knew I was going to need bandages afterward. Everyone knew I had played against him too, because I had the scars to prove it. Not to mention the taunting of his winnings after each game. Joe was a good sport, and you knew he cared about you - well, at least off the court.

When Joe was diagnosed with cancer, the news hit our church family in a big way. What impacted us more was his outlook on his sickness and life. Joe approached his cancer in faith.

Want to know a secret? Cancer sucks. And when you approach cancer in faith, it still sucks.

But we were able to witness the astounding last few years of Joe's life. He soaked in the simple moments with his family more intentionally, because he knew how fragile life was. He forgave quickly and easily, because he knew time was of the essence. His cancer didn't go away, but it didn't get to take the beauty out of his life; it made his life more beautiful, meaningful, and impactful. Joe still played basketball with all his strength and passion, and he still wouldn't let me win. He stayed his same, scrappy self on the court, but also finished every game with a personal encouragement to me about how God was going to use me one day. He was so intentional to speak life into me, a young and rambunctious middle school boy, because he knew he only had a limited number of moments left to speak life into my soul.

I'm sure Joe's feelings weren't always positive on the inside. I'm sure he was scared, mad, confused, hurt, and angry at times. But Joe's faith gave him a perspective that transcended his feelings and made his life impact so many around him, even in the face of cancer.

There's something I need to tell you about faith and feelings that weren't just true for Joe, but they're true for me and you too. Remember what I said just a few pages ago?

When we live in our feelings, we forfeit our belonging. It's not that others don't want us to be a part of their community; it's that we try to be our own community, because we live life aimlessly and selfishly, pursuing the moment.

It's true. But the opposite is true for faith. When we live in faith, it makes room for us to belong, because people want kindness and positivity in their community. When we live in faith, we live with forgiveness, generosity, humility, joy, patience, and peace all flowing freely to those around us. And those are qualities that breathe life and hope into community. Those are qualities that are byproducts of faith, and they make a space of belonging for humanity. It's not only that others desire you to belong in their communities; it's also that who you are in faith makes a space for others to belong with you in community as well. A life of faith is as welcoming to all as it is attractive to all. Faith always belongs.

Aaron Brewer

NINE
BAGGAGE &
BELONGING

Andrea and I love to travel, especially internationally. When we show up at the airport, we do what everyone else does. We get our tickets and check our bags. We never really know what to expect though. Sometimes checking yourself and your baggage is quite simple, because you followed some promptings in an email the day prior. Sometimes checking yourself and your baggage is quite difficult, even when you followed those same promptings in an email the day prior. You really never know what will happen. We're often guilty of being over the baggage weight limit, because we try to put all of our things into as few bags as possible.

One thing that drives me nuts is thinking that I'm saving some money by booking with a particular airline, only to show up and be additionally charged $50.00 per bag. At that point, what am I going to do? I need what's in those bags, and I'm not going to refuse to pay the fee. After all, I want to go on the trip! Baggage is the most annoying part about traveling. Even if you have a small carry-on, you have to tote it around the terminal, keep it beside you when you eat and use the restroom, and then try to find overhead space to cram it into. There's really just so much stress when it comes to baggage. But we all have it.

Baggage

I met Andrea in 2008. She was a hairstylist working in downtown Winchester, Virginia, not far from my parents' shoe store. My mom's friend, Caryn, had won two coupons at a community raffle for a free haircut and gave one to my mom. After her free haircut, my mom wouldn't stop talking about this preacher's daughter who worked in the salon. She said that I just had to go meet this beautiful girl. All I needed to hear was *beautiful*, and I picked up the phone and called the salon.

Andrea: "Old Town Hair Studio."

Me: "Hi, I'm wondering if I can swing by and schedule a haircut."

Andrea: "You can do that over the phone."

Me: "Well, I'm close by and would really like to see where you're located and put eyes on the place."

Andrea: [Long dramatic pause] "Okay?"

Me: "My name's Aaron. I'll see you soon."

You Don't Have To Believe To Belong

I walked over to the address and made my way up the narrow stairway to the salon, which was located on the second floor of a hundred-year-old house, now used for business. I entered and saw a pair of piercingly mysterious, crystal eyes that met mine for only a split second before looking back down at a scheduling book behind a tall counter. I had only been there a few seconds before knowing beyond all doubt that she was the girl I came to see.

Me: "Hi, I'm Aaron."

Andrea was silent and didn't look up.

Me: "I just called."

Andrea was still silent and didn't look up.

I glanced around to see who else could hear me, and I leaned over the counter to make sure Andrea could see and hear me. She was sitting in a chair behind the counter, still looking at the scheduling book. She finally looked up.

Andrea: "What can I do for you?"

Me: "I'd like to schedule a haircut… with you. I'd like to get on your schedule."

Andrea looked back at the scheduling book and gave me a date and time. Without engaging in any conversation, she said, "See you then."

When I showed up to the appointment a few days later, I realized that she had scheduled me outside of the salon's business hours. I thought she had planned it in order to get to know me a little better, but when I walked in, one of her friends, Dana, was sitting in a waiting chair. I knew she must've invited her friend in case she felt uncomfortable around me one-on-one. She could see right through me. She knew I wasn't there for my hair; I was there for her. She wanted some back-up in case I was a lunatic.

Halfway through the appointment, Dana left, and I could finally exhale. I was hoping it was Andrea who gave her the wink or nod to go, signaling she was comfortable with me. The conversation was fun and flirty, though awkward at times, and I paid her more than double what she charged me for the haircut. She said that it would just have to go toward my next cut, and I took that as her plan to see me again. But just in case, I left my sunglasses behind to ensure that we'd have to meet up again soon. Sure enough, we decided to grab lunch at a sushi restaurant that was right between our workplaces to return my sunglasses. She, of course, wasn't alone. She was with her sister and baby nephew. Even though it wasn't a date, I was just glad to have the opportunity to see and talk with her again. A couple evenings later, she called me and asked if I wanted to join her for dinner at IJ Canns, a local restaurant. I was feeling a surge of confidence since she approached me with the invitation. Again, Dana was with her, but this time Dana's husband, Jason, came along too. Instead of a safety net, I considered this our first double date.

A few nights later, she agreed to let me take her out on our first official date - alone. We went to dinner, and then we went fishing on some private property under the stars. Let me interject that I wasn't planning on catching any fish that night. I was just trying to make it look like we were fishing. I was there solely to catch Andrea. We were both dressed in nice clothes, sitting on the dock, and I had a single line out in the water with a vanilla-oatmeal ball on the hook. That's carp bait. I had fished on that property hundreds of times and rarely caught a carp. You don't eat carp, but they're fun to catch, because they're big and put up a good fight.

We were deep in conversation together while sitting on a soft blanket on the dock, when all of the sudden the bobber on my line disappeared into the water. I reeled in the line, and the fish on the hook was not a carp. It was a catfish. I had never caught a catfish before, but I had always heard that you should be careful taking them off the hook, because they would sting you. I wasn't about to let that happen, so I did the only reasonable thing to get the catfish off the hook. I laid it on the dock, stepped on it with my Dansko shoes, and started yanking on the line as hard as I could. A couple minutes later, I had unintentionally mutilated the fish in ways no one would ever want to witness. Andrea was absolutely mortified and in utter shock. "Take me home," she said. And so I did.

Needless to say, that was not the way the date was supposed to end. I couldn't believe it when she agreed to go back out with me. This time we stayed far away from the fishing pond, and we finished the night watching a movie at her place. And we kissed. It was a good night.

Four months later, we were engaged. I guess it's true: *When you know, you know.*

Part of our engagement was premarital counseling. I was uncomfortable with the idea, because I thought a counselor was going to tell me how I should do everything. Either that or I was going to have to talk about all of my feelings. Nevertheless, it was something we had to do in order for her dad to perform our marriage ceremony. Due to an obvious conflict of interest, we didn't go to her dad for counseling. We instead went to a female Christian counselor, Donna Early, whose office happened to be situated in Andrea's church - which her dad pastored.

It was much to my surprise how relaxed, empowered, and confident the counseling sessions made us feel. It was not at all what I had expected. We didn't talk about my feelings or what I should do. We didn't talk about Andrea's feelings or what she should do. Instead, the vast majority of the conversations had to do with our upbringings. We talked about how my parents parented and how her parents parented. We discussed how we might parent together. We talked about the roles my parents played at home, like who washed the dishes, cooked, did the laundry, and cleaned. We talked about some of the roles her parents had, like who handled the finances, cared for the family, and went into the workplace. When we began to realize that Donna was trying to get us to navigate and communicate our expectations of one another, it helped us understand the importance of forming our own identity together apart from the families we knew. We needed and desired to form our own family.

The biggest takeaway I had from premarital counseling was the unconscious baggage we were both bringing into the relationship. It's not that all of the baggage was bad, it was that even the good baggage was still baggage that needed to be unpacked.

We all carry some things with us into the present from our childhood. Whether it's from a religious upbringing, an abusive upbringing, a healthy upbringing, or a dysfunctional upbringing - we carry it into our present life and relationships. We then experience circumstances in our present life and relationships that add more weight to our baggage. Our baggage unloads itself in ways that sit under the surface, but affect every area of our lives. It creates an unhealthy flow of guilt and shame, or sometimes pride and entitlement. Those traits embed themselves into our thoughts and control how we see the people and situations around us. They act like a megaphone in our heads telling us who we are in stark contrast to who God says we are. Those traits always present themselves in opposition to God's image in us. They tell us we are unloveable when God calls us loved. They tell us we don't belong when God shows us we belong to Him.

Belonging

Baggage complicates belonging. It doesn't dictate the reality of our belonging, but it tells us a false story about our belonging. Even when we come to realize our innate belonging to God, humanity, and self, our baggage releases insecurities that create distance from those in our circle of belonging. We become inwardly focused when we believe our insecurities, which corrodes the relational integrity of our belonging.

My insecurities seem to weigh-in on many of my decisions. I certainly try to not allow them to dictate my decisions, but I do hear their lies when making decisions. This book, for instance, was a process to write. Not just because it took a while to put thoughts to words to paper, but because I could hear the insecurities created by my past in my head. They sounded something like this:

I can't say that about the Bible, or it's going to cut off 20% or more of the people who would read this book.

I wonder what my family and formative spiritual leaders are going to think? Do I really want them to think I'm a heretic?

I know this is controversial, so is it something that really needs to be said? I certainly don't want this writing to close more doors than it will ever open.

I'm a seminary dop-out; I'm not even qualified enough to write a book about this topic.

What if people are disappointed in me?

I'm obviously a people pleaser, and I care way too much about what people think of me. I can already hear your response, "Don't worry about what people think, just be who God called you to be." I know, and I agree. I would tell you the same thing too. Do you want to know why I care so much about what people think about me? *Baggage*. That's right, it's baggage from my childhood that I know is there, and it still unloads itself into my thoughts.

The religious environment I was raised in told me exactly what to believe - and what not to believe. It told me that anyone else who didn't believe what we believed was wrong and going to hell. And every one of our beliefs was straight from the Bible, and every word in the Bible had been orally dictated by God to the writer. So our beliefs were unquestionable. I was taught there was no hope for humanity outside of our narrow understanding of God. The world (the rest of humanity outside of our religion) was our enemy. In a nutshell: only we knew the true God; we were right and heaven-bound; everyone else was wrong and hell-bound; and we had the Bible to prove it.

It was very intimidating to be in the fundamental Christian community. We looked for the approval of those in authority. If we didn't have it, we were doomed. That made our environment clique-ish.

If you didn't already belong, it was tough to find belonging with us. The fast-track to belonging was to attend our church and send your kids or grandkids to our Christian school. If you supported one but not the other, you would be accepted by us, but you wouldn't belong with us. It was also easy to be expelled from the community - not physically, but spiritually and relationally. If your marriage failed, if you were caught drinking, if you were heard cursing, if you read a different translation of the Bible, or if you didn't believe the right doctrine and theology, you would no longer find belonging in our community. That's why it was important to believe the right things and follow the teachings of our spiritual leaders; because if we didn't, not only would we be dangling over the hot flames of hell, we would have to realign our beliefs in order to restore our belonging.

That's the spiritual baggage I, and many others who were raised in ultra-conservative Christian environments, bring into life and relationships. My thinking was shaped to believe if I colored outside the theological and moral lines of our doctrine, I would be damned for all eternity. Do I believe that now? Absolutely not. But it is a constant default in my mind that creates tension between who I was shaped to be and who I know God created me to be - not just as an individual, but as a human. My spiritual baggage fosters insecurities that make me question my experience and understanding of God, while motivating me to make decisions in a spirit of fear. That's how I find my balance and grounding. If I'm making decisions based on fear, those decisions aren't grounded in God and won't lead me to a fulfilled life. God doesn't give humans a spirit of fear; instead, He gives us a spirit of love. Decisions made from a spirit of love are always the right decision. Andrea helps me so much in this area, and having someone on my side who understands and challenges me through it is such a blessing.

We don't just wrestle with spiritual baggage, though. Most of us have relational baggage too. Social baggage, personal baggage, mental baggage, and even sinful baggage also plague us. We may not have been able to control much of the baggage that we carry; but if we're honest with ourselves, we all carry a little (or much) baggage that our selfish and wrongful decisions created. We have hurts, habits, and hang-ups that are now part of our reality, whether we like it or not. Instead of ignoring them and hoping they disappear, we must recognize them, give them to God, and allow Him to use them for our betterment.

Our baggage, when unattended to, often puts the worst version of ourselves on display. Although most people want to overlook our baggage in order to create a space for us to belong, we are often the ones who can't overlook our baggage. When we give way to the insecurities from our baggage, we find it difficult to belong anywhere, especially with ourselves.

This is the tricky part about belonging. If we never discover belonging within ourselves, we'll never be able to find true belonging anywhere else. Our self-rejection will ultimately sabotage the relationships we have, isolating us into a life of perpetual loneliness. But when we discover belonging within ourselves, we are able to create a space to belong for those around us. When we are able to love ourselves for who we truly are, forgive ourselves for who we were, and see ourselves for who God has called us to be, we will be able to do the same for others. Belonging isn't something we search for and find around us; it's often something we discover within us.

Belonging is for everyone. It's not just for the accomplished, the likeable, the popular, the athletic, the beautiful, the rich, or the famous. Belonging is for everyone, and it starts within everyone. When you discover it within you, you create it for those around you. So bring on the celebrities and the outcasts, the sinners and the saints, the believers and the non-believers, the conservatives and the liberals. Bring on every race and ethnicity, every gender and sexuality, and every human on the planet. And don't forget to bring your baggage too. We have room for you and all of your stuff. You belong here, and you belong with us; because we belong to each other, and we belong to God.

CONNECT WITH AARON

I'd love to connect with you along your own faith journey to be of any encouragement and help. The best way to connect with me is on social media.

Instagram: @aaronbrewer + @freshfaithorg
Facebook: @freshfaithorg
Twitter: @aaronbrewer
YouTube: @freshfaith

Another way to connect with me is by email at aaron@freshfaith.org or by visiting FreshFaith.org.

#HashTag

Thanks so much for reading this book. It took me over a year to complete it, and I'm grateful to share it with you. I pray it helps you along your journey. If it does, I'd be honored if you would share it with your friends. When posting to social, use the hashtag *#YouDontHaveToBelieveToBelong* to join in and share the journey with others.

Made in the USA
Columbia, SC
21 June 2021